W9-CJC-946

THE WAY TO RAINY MOUNTAIN

THE WAY T

WESTFIELD MEMORIAL LIBRARY
WESTFIELD, NEW JERSEY

AINY MOUNTAIN

N. SCOTT MOMADAY

Illustrated by AL MOMADAY

UNIVERSITY OF NEW MEXICO PRESS

970.3
Mom
100177

ACKNOWLEDGMENTS

The Introduction to this book first appeared in *The Reporter* for January 26, 1967. In slightly different form, it was incorporated in the text of my novel *House Made of Dawn*, published by Harper & Row in 1968.

I wish also to acknowledge my own book, *The Journey of Tai-me*, which is in a special sense the archetype of the present volume. The earlier work was produced in collaboration with D. E. Carlsen and Bruce S. McCurdy at the University of California, Santa Barbara, in a fine edition limited to 100 hand-printed copies.

Finally I should like here to thank those of my kinsmen who willingly recounted to me the tribal history and literature which informs this book.

© The University of New Mexico Press, 1969. *All rights reserved*. Printed in the United States of America by the University of New Mexico Printing Plant, Albuquerque. *Library of Congress Catalog Card No. 69-19154. First edition.*
Second printing

FOR AL AND NATACHEE

WESTFIELD MEMORIAL LIBRARY
WESTFIELD, NEW JERSEY

CONTENTS

THE WAY TO RAINY MOUNTAIN

WESTERN COLLEGE
MIAMI UNIVERSITY

HEADWATERS

Noon in the intermountain plain:
There is scant telling of the marsh—
A log, hollow and weather-stained,
An insect at the mouth, and moss—
Yet waters rise against the roots,
Stand brimming to the stalks. What moves?
What moves on this archaic force
Was wild and welling at the source.

PROLOGUE

The journey began one day long ago on the edge of the northern Plains. It was carried on over a course of many generations and many hundreds of miles. In the end there were many things to remember, to dwell upon and talk about.

"You know, everything had to begin. . . ." For the Kiowas the beginning was a struggle for existence in the bleak northern mountains. It was there, they say, that they entered the world through a hollow log. The end, too, was a struggle, and it was lost. The young Plains culture of the Kiowas withered and died like grass that is burned in the prairie wind. There came a day like destiny; in every direction, as far as the eye could see, carrion lay out in the land. The buffalo was the animal representation of the sun, the essential and sacrificial victim of the Sun Dance. When the wild herds were destroyed, so too was the will of the Kiowa people; there was nothing to sustain them in spirit. But these are idle recollections, the mean and ordinary agonies of human history. The interim was a time of great adventure and nobility and fulfillment.

Tai-me came to the Kiowas in a vision born of suffering and despair. "Take me with you," Tai-me said, "and I will give you whatever you want." And it was so. The great adventure of the Kiowas was a going forth into the heart of the continent. They began a long migration from the headwaters of the Yellowstone River eastward to the Black Hills and south to the Wichita Mountains. Along the way they acquired horses, the religion of the Plains, a love and possession of the open land. Their nomadic soul was set free. In alliance with the Comanches they held dominion in the southern Plains for a hundred years. In the course of that long migration they had come of age as a people. They had conceived a good idea of themselves; they had dared to imagine and determine who they were.

In one sense, then, the way to Rainy Mountain is preeminently the history of an idea, man's idea of himself, and it has old and essential being in language. The verbal tradition by which it has been preserved has suffered a deterioration in time. What remains is fragmentary: mythology, legend, lore, and hearsay—and of course the idea itself, as crucial and complete as it ever was. That is the miracle.

The journey herein recalled continues to be made anew each time the miracle comes to mind, for that is peculiarly the right and responsibility of the imagination. It is a whole journey, intricate with motion and meaning; and it is made with the whole memory, that experience of the mind which is legendary as well as historical, personal as well as cultural. And the journey is an evocation of three things in particular: a landscape that is incomparable, a time that is gone forever, and the human spirit, which endures. The imaginative experience and the historical express equally the traditions of man's reality. Finally, then, the journey recalled is among other things the revelation of one way in which these traditions are conceived, developed, and interfused in the human mind. There are on the way to Rainy Mountain many landmarks, many journeys in the one. From the beginning the migration of the Kiowas was an expression of the human spirit, and that expression is most truly made in terms of wonder and delight: "There were many people, and oh, it was beautiful. That was the beginning of the Sun Dance. It was all for Tai-me, you know, and it was a long time ago."

INTRODUCTION

A single knoll rises out of the plain in Oklahoma, north and west of the Wichita Range. For my people, the Kiowas, it is an old landmark, and they gave it the name Rainy Mountain. The hardest weather in the world is there. Winter brings blizzards, hot tornadic winds arise in the spring, and in summer the prairie is an anvil's edge. The grass turns brittle and brown, and it cracks beneath your feet. There are green belts along the rivers and creeks, linear groves of hickory and pecan, willow and witch hazel. At a distance in July or August the steaming foliage seems almost to writhe in fire. Great green and yellow grasshoppers are everywhere in the tall grass, popping up like corn to sting the flesh, and tortoises crawl about on the red earth, going nowhere in the plenty of time. Loneliness is an aspect of the land. All things in the plain are isolate; there is no confusion of objects in the eye, but one hill or one tree or one man. To look upon that landscape in the early morning, with the sun at your back, is to lose the sense of proportion. Your imagination comes to life, and this, you think, is where Creation was begun.

I returned to Rainy Mountain in July. My grandmother had died in the spring, and I wanted to be at her grave. She had lived to be very old and at last infirm. Her only living daughter was with her when she died, and I was told that in death her face was that of a child.

I like to think of her as a child. When she was born, the Kiowas were living the last great moment of their history. For more than a hundred years they had controlled the open range from the Smoky Hill River to the Red, from the headwaters of the Canadian to the fork of the Arkansas and Cimarron. In alliance with the Comanches, they had ruled the whole of the southern Plains. War was their sacred business, and they were among the finest horsemen the world has ever known. But warfare for the Kiowas was pre-eminently a matter of disposition rather than of survival, and they never understood the grim, unrelenting advance of the U.S. Cavalry. When at last, divided and ill-provisioned, they were driven onto the Staked Plains in the cold rains of autumn, they fell into panic. In Palo Duro Canyon they abandoned their crucial stores to pillage and had nothing then but their lives. In order to save themselves, they surrendered to the soldiers at Fort Sill and were imprisoned in the old stone corral that now stands as a military museum. My grandmother was spared the humiliation of those high gray walls by eight or ten years, but she must have known from birth the affliction of defeat, the dark brooding of old warriors.

Her name was Aho, and she belonged to the last culture to evolve in North America. Her forebears came down from the high country in western Montana nearly three centuries ago. They were a mountain people, a mysterious tribe of hunters whose language has never been positively classified in any major group. In the late seventeenth century they began a long migration to the south and east. It was a journey toward the dawn, and it led to a golden age. Along the way the Kiowas were befriended by the Crows, who gave them the culture and religion of the Plains. They acquired horses, and their ancient nomadic spirit was suddenly free of the ground. They acquired Tai-me, the sacred Sun Dance doll, from that moment the object and symbol of their worship, and so shared in the divinity of the sun. Not least, they acquired the sense of destiny, therefore courage and pride. When they en-

6

tered upon the southern Plains they had been transformed. No longer were they slaves to the simple necessity of survival; they were a lordly and dangerous society of fighters and thieves, hunters and priests of the sun. According to their origin myth, they entered the world through a hollow log. From one point of view, their migration was the fruit of an old prophecy, for indeed they emerged from a sunless world.

Although my grandmother lived out her long life in the shadow of Rainy Mountain, the immense landscape of the continental interior lay like memory in her blood. She could tell of the Crows, whom she had never seen, and of the Black Hills, where she had never been. I wanted to see in reality what she had seen more perfectly in the mind's eye, and traveled fifteen hundred miles to begin my pilgrimage.

Yellowstone, it seemed to me, was the top of the world, a region of deep lakes and dark timber, canyons and waterfalls. But, beautiful as it is, one might have the sense of confinement there. The skyline in all directions is close at hand, the high wall of the woods and deep cleavages of shade. There is a perfect freedom in the mountains, but it belongs to the eagle and the elk, the badger and the bear. The Kiowas reckoned their stature by the distance they could see, and they were bent and blind in the wilderness.

Descending eastward, the highland meadows are a stairway to the plain. In July the inland slope of the Rockies is luxuriant with flax and buckwheat, stonecrop and larkspur. The earth unfolds and the limit of the land recedes. Clusters of trees, and animals grazing far in the distance, cause the vision to reach away and wonder to build upon the mind. The sun follows a longer course in the day, and the sky is immense beyond all comparison. The great billowing clouds that sail upon it are shadows that move upon the grain like water, dividing light. Farther down, in the land of the Crows and Blackfeet, the plain is yellow. Sweet clover takes hold of the hills and bends upon itself to cover and seal the soil. There the Kiowas paused on their way; they had come to the place where they must change their lives. The sun is at home on the plains. Precisely there does it have the certain character of a god. When the Kiowas came to the land of the Crows, they could see the dark lees of the hills at dawn across the Bighorn River, the profusion of light on the grain shelves, the oldest deity ranging after the solstices. Not yet would they veer southward to the caldron of the land that lay below; they must wean their blood from the northern winter and hold the mountains a while longer in their view. They bore Tai-me in procession to the east.

A dark mist lay over the Black Hills, and the land was like iron. At the top of a ridge I caught sight of Devil's Tower upthrust against the gray sky as if in the birth of time the core of the earth had broken through its crust and the motion of the world was begun. There are things in nature that engender an awful quiet in the heart of man; Devil's Tower is one of them. Two centuries ago, because they could not do otherwise, the Kiowas made a legend at the base of the rock. My grandmother said:

Eight children were there at play, seven sisters and their brother. Suddenly the boy was struck dumb; he trembled and began to run upon his hands and feet. His fingers became claws, and his body was covered with fur. Directly there was a bear where the boy had been. The sisters were terrified; they ran, and the bear after them. They came to the stump of a great tree, and the tree spoke to them. It bade them climb upon it, and as they did so it began to rise into the air. The bear came to kill them, but they were just beyond its reach. It reared against the tree and scored the bark all around with its claws. The seven sisters were borne into the sky, and they became the stars of the Big Dipper.

From that moment, and so long as the legend lives, the Kiowas have kinsmen in the night sky. Whatever they were in the mountains, they could be no more. However tenuous their well-being, however much they had suffered and would suffer again, they had found a way out of the wilderness.

My grandmother had a reverence for the sun, a holy regard that now is all but gone out of mankind. There was a wariness in her, and an ancient awe. She was a Christian in her later years, but she had come a long way about, and she never forgot her birthright. As a child she had been to the Sun Dances; she had taken part in those annual rites, and by them she had learned the restoration of her people in the presence of Tai-me. She was about seven when

the last Kiowa Sun Dance was held in 1887 on the Washita River above Rainy Mountain Creek. The buffalo were gone. In order to consummate the ancient sacrifice—to impale the head of a buffalo bull upon the medicine tree—a delegation of old men journeyed into Texas, there to beg and barter for an animal from the Goodnight herd. She was ten when the Kiowas came together for the last time as a living Sun Dance culture. They could find no buffalo; they had to hang an old hide from the sacred tree. Before the dance could begin, a company of soldiers rode out from Fort Sill under orders to disperse the tribe. Forbidden without cause the essential act of their faith, having seen the wild herds slaughtered and left to rot upon the ground, the Kiowas backed away forever from the medicine tree. That was July 20, 1890, at the great bend of the Washita. My grandmother was there. Without bitterness, and for as long as she lived, she bore a vision of deicide.

Now that I can have her only in memory, I see my grandmother in the several postures that were peculiar to her: standing at the wood stove on a winter morning and turning meat in a great iron skillet; sitting at the south window, bent above her beadwork, and afterwards, when her vision failed, looking down for a long time into the fold of her hands; going out upon a cane, very slowly as she did when the weight of age came upon her; praying. I remember her most often at prayer. She made long, rambling prayers out of suffering and hope, having seen many things. I was never sure that I had the right to hear, so exclusive were they of all mere custom and company. The last time I saw her she prayed standing by the side of her bed at night, naked to the waist, the light of a kerosene lamp moving upon her dark skin. Her long, black hair, always drawn and braided in the day, lay upon her shoulders and against her breasts like a shawl. I do not speak Kiowa, and I never understood her prayers, but there was something inherently sad in the sound, some merest hesitation upon the syllables of sorrow. She began in a high and descending pitch, exhausting her breath to silence; then again and again—and always the same intensity of effort, of something that is, and is not, like urgency in the human voice. Transported so in the dancing light among the shadows of her room, she seemed beyond the reach of time. But that was illusion; I think I knew then that I should not see her again.

Houses are like sentinels in the plain, old keepers of the weather watch. There, in a very little while, wood takes on the appearance of great age. All colors wear soon away in the wind and rain, and then the wood is burned gray and the grain appears and the nails turn red with rust. The windowpanes are black and opaque; you imagine there is nothing within, and indeed there are many ghosts, bones given up to the land. They stand here and there against the sky, and you approach them for a longer time than you expect. They belong in the distance; it is their domain.

Once there was a lot of sound in my grandmother's house, a lot of coming and going, feasting and talk. The summers there were full of excitement and reunion. The Kiowas are a summer people; they abide the cold and keep to themselves, but when the season turns and the land becomes warm and vital they cannot hold still; an old love of going returns upon them. The aged visitors who came to my grandmother's house when I was a child were made of lean and leather, and they bore themselves upright. They wore great black hats and bright ample shirts that shook in the wind. They rubbed fat upon their hair and wound their braids with strips of colored cloth. Some of them painted their faces and carried the scars of old and cherished enmities. They were an old council of warlords, come to remind and be reminded of who they were. Their wives and daughters served them well. The women might indulge themselves; gossip was at once the mark and compensation of their servitude. They made loud and elaborate talk among themselves, full of jest and gesture, fright and false alarm. They went abroad in fringed and flowered shawls, bright beadwork and German silver. They were at home in the kitchen, and they prepared meals that were banquets.

There were frequent prayer meetings, and great nocturnal feasts. When I was a child I played with my cousins outside, where the lamplight fell upon the ground and the singing of the old people rose up around us and carried away into the darkness. There were a lot of good things to eat, a lot of laughter and surprise. And afterwards, when the quiet returned, I lay down with my grandmother and could hear the frogs away by the river and feel the motion of the air.

Now there is a funeral silence in the rooms, the endless wake of some final word. The walls have closed in upon my grandmother's house. When I returned to it in mourning, I saw for the first time in my life how small it was. It was late at night, and there was a white moon, nearly full. I sat for a long time on the stone steps by the kitchen door. From there I could see out across the land; I could see the long row of trees by the creek, the low light upon the rolling plains, and the stars of the Big Dipper. Once I looked at the moon and caught sight of a strange thing. A cricket had perched upon the handrail, only a few inches away from me. My line of vision was such that the creature filled the moon like a fossil. It had gone there, I thought, to live and die, for there, of all places, was its small definition made whole and eternal. A warm wind rose up and purled like the longing within me.

The next morning I awoke at dawn and went out on the dirt road to Rainy Mountain. It was already hot, and the grasshoppers began to fill the air. Still, it was early in the morning, and the birds sang out of the shadows. The long yellow grass on the mountain shone in the bright light, and a scissortail hied above the land. There, where it ought to be, at the end of a long and legendary way, was my grandmother's grave. Here and there on the dark stones were ancestral names. Looking back once, I saw the mountain and came away.

THE SETTING OUT

I

You know, everything had to begin, and this is how it was: the Kiowas came one by one into the world through a hollow log. They were many more than now, but not all of them got out. There was a woman whose body was swollen up with child, and she got stuck in the log. After that, no one could get through, and that is why the Kiowas are a small tribe in number. They looked all around and saw the world. It made them glad to see so many things. They called themselves *Kwuda,* "coming out."

They called themselves Kwuda and later Tepda, both of which mean "coming out." And later still they took the name Gaigwu, a name which can be taken to indicate something of which the two halves differ from each other in appearance. It was once a custom among Kiowa warriors that they cut their hair on the right side of the head only and on a line level with the lobe of the ear, while on the left they let the hair grow long and wore it in a thick braid wrapped in otter skin. "Kiowa" is indicated in sign language by holding the hand palm up and slightly cupped to the right side of the head and rotating it back and forth from the wrist. "Kiowa" is thought to derive from the softened Comanche form of Gaigwu.

I remember coming out upon the northern Great Plains in the late spring. There were meadows of blue and yellow wild-flowers on the slopes, and I could see the still, sunlit plain below, reaching away out of sight. At first there is no discrimination in the eye, nothing but the land itself, whole and impenetrable. But then smallest things begin to stand out of the depths— herds and rivers and groves—and each of these has perfect being in terms of distance and of silence and of age. Yes, I thought, now I see the earth as it really is; never again will I see things as I saw them yesterday or the day before.

II

They were going along, and some were hunting. An antelope was killed and quartered in the meadow. Well, one of the big chiefs came up and took the udders of that animal for himself, but another big chief wanted those udders also, and there was a great quarrel between them. Then, in anger, one of these chiefs gathered all of his followers together and went away. They are called *Azatanhop,* "the udder-angry travelers off." No one knows where they went or what happened to them.

This is one of the oldest memories of the tribe. There have been reports of a people in the Northwest who speak a language that is similar to Kiowa.

In the winter of 1848-49, the buffalo ranged away from easy reach, and food was scarce. There was an antelope drive in the vicinity of Bent's Fort, Colorado. According to ancient custom, antelope medicine was made, and the Kiowas set out on foot and on horseback—men, women, and children—after game. They formed a great circle, inclosing a large area of the plain, and began to converge upon the center. By this means antelope and other animals were trapped and killed, often with clubs and even with the bare hands. By necessity were the Kiowas reminded of their ancient ways.

One morning on the high plains of Wyoming I saw several pronghorns in the distance. They were moving very slowly at an angle away from me, and they were almost invisible in the tall brown and yellow grass. They ambled along in their own wilderness dimension of time, as if no notion of flight could ever come upon them. But I remembered once having seen a frightened buck on the run, how the white rosette of its rump seemed to hang for the smallest fraction of time at the top of each frantic bound—like a succession of sunbursts against the purple hills.

III

Before there were horses the Kiowas had need of dogs. That was a long time ago, when dogs could talk. There was a man who lived alone; he had been thrown away, and he made his camp here and there on the high ground. Now it was dangerous to be alone, for there were enemies all around. The man spent his arrows hunting food. He had one arrow left, and he shot a bear; but the bear was only wounded and it ran away. The man wondered what to do. Then a dog came up to him and said that many enemies were coming; they were close by and all around. The man could think of no way to save himself. But the dog said: "You know, I have puppies. They are young and weak and they have nothing to eat. If you will take care of my puppies, I will show you how to get away." The dog led the man here and there, around and around, and they came to safety.

A hundred years ago the Comanche Ten Bears remarked upon the great number of horses which the Kiowas owned. "When we first knew you," he said, "you had nothing but dogs and sleds." It was so; the dog is primordial. Perhaps it was dreamed into being.

The principal warrior society of the Kiowas was the Ka-itsenko, "Real Dogs," and it was made up of ten men only, the ten most brave. Each of these men wore a long ceremonial sash and carried a sacred arrow. In time of battle he must by means of this arrow impale the end of his sash to the earth and stand his ground to the death. Tradition has it that the founder of the Ka-itsenko had a dream in which he saw a band of warriors, outfitted after the fashion of the society, being led by a dog. The dog sang the song of the Ka-itsenko, then said to the dreamer: "You are a dog; make a noise like a dog and sing a dog song."

There were always dogs about my grandmother's house. Some of them were nameless and lived a life of their own. They belonged there in a sense that the word "ownership" does not include. The old people paid them scarcely any attention, but they should have been sad, I think, to see them go.

IV

They lived at first in the mountains. They did not yet know of
Tai-me, but this is what they knew: There was a man and his wife.
They had a beautiful child, a little girl whom they would not
allow to go out of their sight. But one day a friend of the family
came and asked if she might take the child outside to play. The
mother guessed that would be all right, but she told the friend to
leave the child in its cradle and to place the cradle in a tree. While
the child was in the tree, a redbird came among the branches. It
was not like any bird that you have seen; it was very beautiful, and
it did not fly away. It kept still upon a limb, close to the child.
After a while the child got out of its cradle and began to climb
after the redbird. And at the same time the tree began to grow
taller, and the child was borne up into the sky. She was then a
woman, and she found herself in a strange place. Instead of a
redbird, there was a young man standing before her. The man
spoke to her and said: "I have been watching you for a long time,
and I knew that I would find a way to bring you here. I have
brought you here to be my wife." The woman looked all around;
she saw that he was the only living man there. She saw that he was
the sun.

There the land itself ascends into the sky. These mountains lie at the top of the continent, and they cast a long rain shadow on the sea of grasses to the east. They arise out of the last North American wilderness, and they have wilderness names: Wasatch, Bitterroot, Bighorn, Wind River.

I have walked in a mountain meadow bright with Indian paintbrush, lupine, and wild buckwheat, and I have seen high in the branches of a lodgepole pine the male pine grosbeak, round and rose-colored, its dark, striped wings nearly invisible in the soft, mottled light. And the uppermost branches of the tree seemed very slowly to ride across the blue sky.

V

After that the woman grew lonely. She thought about her people, and she wondered how they were getting on. One day she had a quarrel with the sun, and the sun went away. In her anger she dug up the root of a bush which the sun had warned her never to go near. A piece of earth fell from the root, and she could see her people far below. By that time she had given birth; she had a child—a boy by the sun. She made a rope out of sinew and took her child upon her back; she climbed down upon the rope, but when she came to the end, her people were still a long way off, and there she waited with her child on her back. It was evening; the sun came home and found his woman gone. At once he thought of the bush and went to the place where it had grown. There he saw the woman and the child, hanging by the rope half way down to the earth. He was very angry, and he took up a ring, a gaming wheel, in his hand. He told the ring to follow the rope and strike the woman dead. Then he threw the ring and it did what he told it to do; it struck the woman and killed her, and then the sun's child was all alone.

The plant is said to have been the pomme blanche, or pomme de prairie, of the voyageurs, whose chronicles refer time and again to its use by the Indians. It grows on the high plains and has a farinaceous root that is turnip-like in taste and in shape. This root is a healthful food, and attempts have been made to cultivate the plant as a substitute for the potato.

The anthropologist Mooney wrote in 1896: "Unlike the neighboring Cheyenne and Arapaho, who yet remember that they once lived east of the Missouri and cultivated corn, the Kiowa have no tradition of ever having been an agricultural people or anything but a tribe of hunters."

Even now they are meateaters; I think it is not in them to be farmers. My grandfather, Mammedaty, worked hard to make wheat and cotton grow on his land, but it came to very little in the end. Once when I was a small boy I went across the creek to the house where the old woman Keahdinekeah lived. Some men and boys came in from the pasture, where a calf had just been killed and butchered. One of the boys held the calf's liver—still warm and wet with life—in his hand, eating of it with great relish. I have heard that the old hunters of the Plains prized the raw liver and tongue of the buffalo above all other delicacies.

VI

The sun's child was big enough to walk around on the earth, and he saw a camp nearby. He made his way to it and saw that a great spider—that which is called a grandmother—lived there. The spider spoke to the sun's child, and the child was afraid. The grandmother was full of resentment; she was jealous, you see, for the child had not yet been weaned from its mother's breasts. She wondered whether the child were a boy or a girl, and therefore she made two things, a pretty ball and a bow and arrows. These things she left alone with the child all the next day. When she returned, she saw that the ball was full of arrows, and she knew then that the child was a boy and that he would be hard to raise. Time and again the grandmother tried to capture the boy, but he always ran away. Then one day she made a snare out of rope. The boy was caught up in the snare, and he cried and cried, but the grandmother sang to him and at last he fell asleep.

> Go to sleep and do not cry.
> Your mother is dead, and still you feed
> upon her breasts.
> Oo-oo-la-la-la-la, oo-oo.

In the autumn of 1874, the Kiowas were driven southward towards the Staked Plains. Columns of troops were converging upon them from all sides, and they were bone-weary and afraid. They camped on Elk Creek, and the next day it began to rain. It rained hard all that day, and the Kiowas waited on horseback for the weather to clear. Then, as evening came on, the earth was suddenly crawling with spiders, great black tarantulas, swarming on the flood.

I know of spiders. There are dirt roads in the Plains. You see them, and you wonder where and how far they go. They seem very old and untraveled, as if they all led away to deserted houses. But creatures cross these roads: dung beetles and grasshoppers, sidewinders and tortoises. Now and then there comes a tarantula, at evening, always larger than you imagine, dull and dark brown, covered with long, dusty hairs. There is something crochety about them; they stop and go and angle away.

always larger than you imagine, dull and dark brown.

VII

The years went by, and the boy still had the ring which killed his mother. The grandmother spider told him never to throw the ring into the sky, but one day he threw it up, and it fell squarely on top of his head and cut him in two. He looked around, and there was another boy, just like himself, his twin. The two of them laughed and laughed, and then they went to the grandmother spider. She nearly cried aloud when she saw them, for it had been hard enough to raise the one. Even so, she cared for them well and made them fine clothes to wear.

Mammedaty owned horses. And he could remember that it was essentially good to own horses, that it was hard to be without horses. There was a day: Mammedaty got down from a horse for the last time. Of all the tribes of the Plains, the Kiowas owned the greatest number of horses per person.

On summer afternoons I went swimming in the Washita River. The current was slow, and the warm, brown water seemed to be standing still. It was a secret place. There in the deep shade, inclosed in the dense, overhanging growth of the banks, my mind fixed on the wings of a dragonfly or the flitting motion of a water strider, the great open land beyond was all but impossible to imagine. But it was there, a stone's throw away. Once, from the limb of a tree, I saw myself in the brown water; then a frog leaped from the bank, breaking the image apart.

VIII

Now each of the twins had a ring, and the grandmother spider told
them never to throw the rings into the sky. But one day they threw
them up into the high wind. The rings rolled over a hill, and the
twins ran after them. They ran beyond the top of the hill and fell
down into the mouth of a cave. There lived a giant and his wife.
The giant had killed a lot of people in the past by building fires
and filling the cave with smoke, so that the people could not
breathe. Then the twins remembered something that the grandmother spider had told them: "If ever you get caught in the cave,
say to yourselves the word *thain-mom*, 'above my eyes.' " When
the giant began to set fires around, the twins repeated the word
thain-mom over and over to themselves, and the smoke remained
above their eyes. When the giant had made three great clouds of
smoke, his wife saw that the twins sat without coughing or crying,
and she became frightened. "Let them go," she said, "or something
bad will happen to us." The twins took up their rings and returned
to the grandmother spider. She was glad to see them.

A word has power in and of itself. It comes from nothing into sound and meaning; it gives origin to all things. By means of words can a man deal with the world on equal terms. And the word is sacred. A man's name is his own; he can keep it or give it away as he likes. Until recent times, the Kiowas would not speak the name of a dead man. To do so would have been disrespectful and dishonest. The dead take their names with them out of the world.

When Aho saw or heard or thought of something bad, she said the word zei-dl-bei, "frightful." It was the one word with which she confronted evil and the incomprehensible. I liked her to say it, for she screwed up her face in a wonderful look of displeasure and clicked her tongue. It was not an exclamation so much, I think, as it was a warding off, an exertion of language upon ignorance and disorder.

IX

The next thing that happened to the twins was this: They killed a great snake which they found in their tipi. When they told the grandmother spider what they had done, she cried and cried. They had killed their grandfather, she said. And after that the grandmother spider died. The twins wrapped her in a hide and covered her with leaves by the water. The twins lived on for a long time, and they were greatly honored among the Kiowas.

In another and perhaps older version of the story, it is a porcupine and not a redbird that is the representation of the sun. In that version, too, one of the twins is said to have walked into the waters of a lake and disappeared forever, while the other at last transformed himself into ten portions of "medicine," thereby giving of his own body in eucharistic form to the Kiowas. The ten bundles of the talyi-da-i, "boy medicine" are, like the Tai-me, chief objects of religious veneration.

When he was a boy, my father went with his grandmother, Keahdinekeah, to the shrine of one of the talyi-da-i. The old woman made an offering of bright cloth, and she prayed. The shrine was a small, specially-made tipi; inside, suspended from the lashing of the poles, was the medicine itself. My father knew that it was very powerful, and the very sight of it filled him with wonder and regard. The holiness of such a thing can be imparted to the human spirit, I believe, for I remember that it shone in the sightless eyes of Keahdinekeah. Once I was taken to see her at the old house on the other side of Rainy Mountain Creek. The room was dark, and her old age filled it like a substance. She was white-haired and blind, and, in that strange reversion that comes upon the very old, her skin was as soft as the skin of a baby. I remember the sound of her glad weeping and the water-like touch of her hand.

X

Long ago there were bad times. The Kiowas were hungry and there was no food. There was a man who heard his children cry from hunger, and he went out to look for food. He walked four days and became very weak. On the fourth day he came to a great canyon. Suddenly there was thunder and lightning. A voice spoke to him and said, "Why are you following me? What do you want?" The man was afraid. The thing standing before him had the feet of a deer, and its body was covered with feathers. The man answered that the Kiowas were hungry. "Take me with you," the voice said, "and I will give you whatever you want." From that day Tai-me has belonged to the Kiowas.

The great central figure of the kado, or Sun Dance, ceremony is the taime. This is a small image, less than 2 feet in length, representing a human figure dressed in a robe of white feathers, with a headdress consisting of a single upright feather and pendants of ermine skin, with numerous strands of blue beads around its neck, and painted upon the face, breast, and back with designs symbolic of the sun and moon. The image itself is of dark-green stone, in form rudely resembling a human head and bust, probably shaped by art like the stone fetishes of the Pueblo tribes. It is preserved in a rawhide box in charge of the hereditary keeper, and is never under any circumstances exposed to view except at the annual Sun Dance, when it is fastened to a short upright stick planted within the medicine lodge, near the western side. It was last exposed in 1888.—Mooney

Once I went with my father and grandmother to see the Tai-me bundle. It was suspended by means of a strip of ticking from the fork of a small ceremonial tree. I made an offering of bright red cloth, and my grandmother prayed aloud. It seemed a long time that we were there. I had never come into the presence of Tai-me before—nor have I since. There was a great holiness all about in the room, as if an old person had died there or a child had been born.

XI

A long time ago there were two brothers. It was winter, and the buffalo had wandered far away. Food was very scarce. The two brothers were hungry, and they wondered what to do. One of them got up in the early morning and went out, and he found a lot of fresh meat there on the ground in front of the tipi. He was very happy, and he called his brother outside. "Look," he said. "Something very good has happened, and we have plenty of food." But his brother was afraid and said: "This is too strange a thing. I believe that we had better not eat that meat." But the first brother scolded him and said that he was foolish. Then he went ahead and ate of the meat all by himself. In a little while something awful happened to him; he began to change. When it was all over, he was no longer a man; he was some kind of water beast with little short legs and a long, heavy tail. Then he spoke to his brother and said: "You were right, and you must not eat of that meat. Now I must go and live in the water, but we are brothers, and you ought to come and see me now and then." After that the man went down to the water's edge, sometimes, and called his brother out. He told him how things were with the Kiowas.

During the peyote ritual a fire is kept burning in the center of the tipi, inclosed within a crescent-shaped altar. On top of the altar there is a single, sacred peyote. After the chief priest utters the opening prayer, four peyotes are given to each celebrant, who eats them one after another. Then, in turn, each man sings four sacred songs, and all the while there is the sound of the rattle and the drum—and the fitful, many-colored glare of the fire. The songs go on all through the night, broken only by intervals of prayer, additional distributions of peyote, and, at midnight, a peculiar baptismal ceremony.

Mammedaty was a peyote man, and he was therefore distinguished by these things: a necklace of beans, a beaded staff and rattle, an eagle-bone whistle, and a fan made from the feathers of a water bird. He saw things that other men do not see. Once a heavy rain caused the Washita River to overflow and Rainy Mountain Creek to swell and "back up." Mammedaty went to the creek, near the crossing, to swim. And while he was there, the water began strangely to move against him, slowly at first, then fast, in high, hard waves. There was some awful commotion beneath the surface, and Mammedaty got out of the water and ran away. Later he went back to that place. There was a wide swath in the brush of the bank and the tracks of a huge animal, leading down to the water's edge.

WESTFIELD MEMORIAL LIBRARY
WESTFIELD, NEW JERSEY

some awful commotion beneath the surface.

THE GOING ON

XII

An old man there was who lived with his wife and child. One night the woman was pounding meat, and her little son wanted to taste it. She gave him a ball of meat and he went outside to eat it. Then he returned and wanted more. She gave him another ball of meat, and again he went outside. A third time he came and asked for meat. The old man began to be afraid. He told his wife to give the child a large ball of meat and to act as if these things were all right. When the little boy came in again, there was an enemy with him. The enemy said: "There are many of us and we are all around. We came to kill you, but your son has given me food. If you will feed us all, we will not harm you." But the old man did not believe his enemy, and while his wife cooked fat upon the fire he crept out and led their horses upstream. When he was well away, he called out in the voice of a bird. Then the woman knew that it was time to go. She set fire to the fat and threw it all around upon the enemies, who were sitting there; then she took up the little boy in her arms and ran upstream. That is how the old man and the woman and their child got away. From a safe distance they could see the fire and hear the screams of their enemies.

In the winter of 1872-73, a fine heraldic tipi was accidentally destroyed by fire. Known as the Do-giagya guat, "tipi with battle pictures," it was ornamented with fine pictures of fighting men and
arms on one side and wide, horizontal bands of black and yellow
on the other. The Do-giagya guat belonged to the family of the
great chief Dohasan and occupied the second place in the tribal
circle on ceremonial occasions.

There are meadowlarks and quail in the open land. One day
late in the afternoon I walked about among the headstones at
Rainy Mountain Cemetery. The shadows were very long; there
was a deep blush on the sky, and the dark red earth seemed
to glow with the setting sun. For a few moments, at that particular time of the day, there is deep silence. Nothing moves, and
it does not occur to you to make any sound. Something is
going on there in the shadows. Everything has slowed to a
stop in order that the sun might take leave of the land. And
then there is the sudden, piercing call of a bobwhite. The whole
world is startled by it.

XIII

If an arrow is well made, it will have tooth marks upon it. That is how you know. The Kiowas made fine arrows and straightened them in their teeth. Then they drew them to the bow to see if they were straight. Once there was a man and his wife. They were alone at night in their tipi. By the light of the fire the man was making arrows. After a while he caught sight of something. There was a small opening in the tipi where two hides were sewn together. Someone was there on the outside, looking in. The man went on with his work, but he said to his wife: "Someone is standing outside. Do not be afraid. Let us talk easily, as of ordinary things." He took up an arrow and straightened it in his teeth; then, as it was right for him to do, he drew it to the bow and took aim, first in this direction and then in that. And all the while he was talking, as if to his wife. But this is how he spoke: "I know that you are there on the outside, for I can feel your eyes upon me. If you are a Kiowa, you will understand what I am saying, and you will speak your name." But there was no answer, and the man went on in the same way, pointing the arrow all around. At last his aim fell upon the place where his enemy stood, and he let go of the string. The arrow went straight to the enemy's heart.

The old men were the best arrowmakers, for they could bring time and patience to their craft. The young men—the fighters and hunters—were willing to pay a high price for arrows that were well made.

When my father was a boy, an old man used to come to Mammedaty's house and pay his respects. He was a lean old man in braids and was impressive in his age and bearing. His name was Cheney, and he was an arrowmaker. Every morning, my father tells me, Cheney would paint his wrinkled face, go out, and pray aloud to the rising sun. In my mind I can see that man as if he were there now. I like to watch him as he makes his prayer. I know where he stands and where his voice goes on the rolling grasses and where the sun comes up on the land. There, at dawn, you can feel the silence. It is cold and clear and deep like water. It takes hold of you and will not let you go.

WESTFIELD MEMORIAL LIBRARY

WESTFIELD, NEW JERSEY

XIV

The Kiowa language is hard to understand, but, you know, the storm spirit understands it. This is how it was: Long ago the Kiowas decided to make a horse; they decided to make it out of clay, and so they began to shape the clay with their hands. Well, the horse began to be. But it was a terrible, terrible thing. It began to writhe, slowly at first, then faster and faster until there was a great commotion everywhere. The wind grew up and carried everything away; great trees were uprooted, and even the buffalo were thrown up into the sky. The Kiowas were afraid of that awful thing, and they went running about, talking to it. And at last it was calm. Even now, when they see the storm clouds gathering, the Kiowas know what it is: that a strange wild animal roams on the sky. It has the head of a horse and the tail of a great fish. Lightning comes from its mouth, and the tail, whipping and thrashing on the air, makes the high, hot wind of the tornado. But they speak to it, saying "Pass over me." They are not afraid of *Man-ka-ih*, for it understands their language.

At times the plains are bright and calm and quiet; at times they are black with the sudden violence of weather. Always there are winds.

A few feet from the southwest corner of my grandmother's house, there is a storm cellar. It will be there, I think, when the house and the arbor and the barn have disappeared. There are many of those crude shelters in that part of the world. They conform to the shape of the land and are scarcely remarkable: low earthen mounds with heavy wooden trapdoors that appear to open upon the underworld. I have seen the wind drive the rain so hard that a grown man could not open the door against it, and once, descending into that place, I saw the whole land at night become visible and blue and phosphorescent in the flash of lightning.

100177

whipping and thrashing on the air.

XV

Quoetotai was a good-looking young man and a great warrior be-
sides. One of Many Bears' wives fell in love with him, and they
carried on. After that, Quoetotai went out one day. As he was crossing the river, Many Bears came out of a hiding place on the bank
and shot him with an arrow; then he ran away. Quoetotai went
back to the camp and someone pulled the arrow out of him. He
was very sick, and he had lost a lot of blood. The medicine man
worked over him for a long time, and the next day Quoetotai was
all right. You know, he made up his mind to take Many Bears' wife
away. After that, some of the men wanted to raid in Mexico. It was
the custom to have a dance on the night before the men went away.
There was a lot of singing, and now and then someone got up to
say brave things. Many Bears' wife got up and called attention to
herself. She said: "All of you, listen to my song. Something will
happen tonight." Then she sang, and, you know, the old people
still remember her song.

> I am going to leave my belongings,
> I am going to leave my home.
> Again I say it, I am going to leave my son.

Quoetotai took that woman away, and they roamed with the Comanches for fifteen years. When at last they returned to their own
people, Many Bears was the first man to welcome them. "Quoetotai," he said, "from this time on you and I will be brothers. Now
I give you six horses."

The artist George Catlin traveled among the Kiowas in 1834. He observes that they are superior to the Comanches and Wichitas in appearance. They are tall and straight, relaxed and graceful. They have fine, classical features, and in this respect they resemble more closely the tribes of the north than those of the south.

Catlin's portrait of Kotsatoah is the striking figure of a man, tall and lean, yet powerful and fully developed. He is lithe, and he knows beyond any doubt of his great strength and vigor. He stands perfectly at ease, the long drape of his robe flowing with the lines of his body. His left hand rests upon his shield and holds a bow and arrows. His head is set firmly, and there is a look of bemused and infinite tolerance in his eyes. He is said to have been nearly seven feet tall and able to run down and kill a buffalo on foot. I should like to have seen that man, as Catlin saw him, walking toward me, or away in the distance, perhaps, alone and against the sky.

XVI

There was a strange thing, a buffalo with horns of steel. One day a man came upon it in the plain, just there where once upon a time four trees stood close together. The man and the buffalo began to fight. The man's hunting horse was killed right away, and the man climbed one of the trees. The great bull lowered its head and began to strike the tree with its black metal horns, and soon the tree fell. But the man was quick, and he leaped to the safety of the second tree. Again the bull struck with its unnatural horns, and the tree soon splintered and fell. The man leaped to the third tree and all the while he shot arrows at the beast; but the arrows glanced away like sparks from its dark hide. At last there remained only one tree and the man had only one arrow. He believed then that he would surely die. But something spoke to him and said: "Each time the buffalo prepares to charge, it spreads its cloven hooves and strikes the ground. Only there in the cleft of the hoof is it vulnerable; it is there you must aim." The buffalo went away and turned, spreading its hooves, and the man drew the arrow to his bow. His aim was true and the arrow struck deep into the soft flesh of the hoof. The great bull shuddered and fell, and its steel horns flashed once in the sun.

Forty years ago the townspeople of Carnegie, Oklahoma, gathered about two old Kiowa men who were mounted on work horses and armed with bows and arrows. Someone had got a buffalo, a poor broken beast in which there was no trace left of the wild strain. The old men waited silently amid the laughter and talk; then, at a signal, the buffalo was let go. It balked at first, more confused, perhaps, than afraid, and the horses had to be urged and then brought up short. The people shouted, and at last the buffalo wheeled and ran. The old men gave chase, and in the distance they were lost to view in a great, red cloud of dust. But they ran that animal down and killed it with arrows.

One morning my father and I walked in Medicine Park, on the edge of a small herd of buffalo. It was late in the spring, and many of the cows had newborn calves. Nearby a calf lay in the tall grass; it was red-orange in color, delicately beautiful with new life. We approached, but suddenly the cow was there in our way, her great dark head low and fearful-looking. Then she came at us, and we turned and ran as hard as we could. She gave up after a short run, and I think we had not been in any real danger. But the spring morning was deep and beautiful and our hearts were beating fast and we knew just then what it was to be alive.

its steel horns flashed once in the sun.

XVII

Bad women are thrown away. Once there was a handsome young man. He was wild and reckless, and the chief talked to the wind about him. After that, the man went hunting. A great whirlwind passed by, and he was blind. The Kiowas have no need of a blind man; they left him alone with his wife and child. The winter was coming on and food was scarce. In four days the man's wife grew tired of caring for him. A herd of buffalo came near, and the man knew the sound. He asked his wife to hand him a bow and an arrow. "You must tell me," he said, "when the buffalo are directly in front of me." And in that way he killed a bull, but his wife said that he had missed. He asked for another arrow and killed another bull, but again his wife said that he had missed. Now the man was a hunter, and he knew the sound an arrow makes when it strikes home, but he said nothing. Then his wife helped herself to the meat and ran away with her child. The man was blind; he ate grass and kept himself alive. In seven days a band of Kiowas found him and took him to their camp. There in the firelight a woman was telling a story. She told of how her husband had been killed by enemy warriors. The blind man listened, and he knew her voice. That was a bad woman. At sunrise they threw her away.

In the Kiowa calendars there is graphic proof that the lives of women were hard, whether they were "bad women" or not. Only the captives, who were slaves, held lower status. During the Sun Dance of 1843, a man stabbed his wife in the breast because she accepted Chief Dohasan's invitation to ride with him in the ceremonial procession. And in the winter of 1851-52, Big Bow stole the wife of a man who was away on a raiding expedition. He brought her to his father's camp and made her wait outside in the bitter cold while he went in to collect his things. But his father knew what was going on, and he held Big Bow and would not let him go. The woman was made to wait in the snow until her feet were frozen.

Mammedaty's grandmother, Kau-au-ointy, was a Mexican captive, taken from her homeland when she was a child of eight or ten years. I never knew her, but I have been to her grave at Rainy Mountain.

KAU-AU-OINTY

BORN 1834

DIED 1929

AT REST

She raised a lot of eyebrows, they say, for she would not play the part of a Kiowa woman. From slavery she rose up to become a figure in the tribe. She owned a great herd of cattle, and she could ride as well as any man. She had blue eyes.

XVIII

You know, the Kiowas are a summer people. Once upon a time a
group of young men sat down in a circle and spoke of mighty
things. This is what they said: "When the fall of the year comes
around, where does the summer go? Where does it live?" They
decided to follow the sun southward to its home, and so they set
out on horseback. They rode for days and weeks and months,
farther to the south than any Kiowa had ever gone before, and
they saw many strange and wonderful things. At last they came to
the place where they saw the strangest thing of all. Night was coming on, and they were very tired of riding; they made camp in a
great thicket. All but one of them went right to sleep. He was a
good hunter, and he could see well in the moonlight. He caught
sight of something: men were all about in the trees, moving silently from limb to limb. They darted across the face of the full moon,
and he saw that they were small and had tails! He could not believe
his eyes, but the next morning he told the others of what he had
seen. They only laughed at him and told him not to eat such a large
supper again. But later, as they were breaking camp, a certain feeling came over them all at once: they felt that they were being
watched. And when they looked up, the small men with tails began
to race about in the limbs overhead. That is when the Kiowas
turned around and came away; they had had quite enough of that
place. They had found the sun's home after all, they reasoned, and
they were hungry for the good buffalo meat of their homeland.

It is unnecessary to dilate on the revolution made in the life of the Indian by the possession of the horse. Without it he was a half-starved skulker in the timber, creeping up on foot toward the unwary deer or building a brush corral with infinite labor to surround a herd of antelope, and seldom venturing more than a few days' journey from home. With the horse he was transformed into the daring buffalo hunter, able to procure in a single day enough food to supply his family for a year, leaving him free then to sweep the plains with his war parties along a range of a thousand miles.— Mooney

Some of my earliest memories are of the summers on Rainy Mountain Creek, when we lived in the arbor, on the north side of my grandmother's house. From there you could see downhill to the pecan grove, the dense, dark growth along the water, and beyond, the long sweep of the earth itself, curving out on the sky. The arbor was open on all sides to the light and the air and the sounds of the land. You could see far and wide even at night, by the light of the moon; there was nothing to stand in your way. And when the season turned and it was necessary to move back into the house, there was a sense of confinement and depression for a time. Now and then in winter, when I passed by the arbor on my way to draw water at the well, I looked inside and thought of the summer. The hard dirt floor was dark red in color—the color of pipestone.

he was transformed into a daring buffalo hunter.

THE CLOSING IN

XIX

On a raid against the Utes, one of two brothers was captured. The other, alone and of his own will, stole into the Ute camp and tried to set his brother free, but he too was captured. The chief of the Utes had respect for the man's bravery, and he made a bargain with him. If he could carry his brother on his back and walk upon a row of greased buffalo heads without falling to the ground, both brothers would be given horses and allowed to return in safety to their home. The man bore his brother on his back and walked upon the heads of the buffalo and kept his footing. The Ute chief was true to his word, and the brothers returned to their own people on horseback.

After the fight at Palo Duro Canyon, the Kiowas came in, a few at
a time, to surrender at Fort Sill. Their horses and weapons were
confiscated, and they were imprisoned. In a field just west of the
post, the Indian ponies were destroyed. Nearly 800 horses were
killed outright; two thousand more were sold, stolen, given away.

SUMMER 1879

Tsen-pia Kado, "Horse-eating sun dance." It is indicated on the
Set-tan calendar by the figure of a horse's head above the medicine
lodge. This dance was held on Elm Fork of Red River, and was so
called because the buffalo had now become so scarce that the
Kiowa, who had gone on their regular hunt the preceding winter,
had found so few that they were obliged to kill and eat their ponies
during the summer to save themselves from starving. This may be
recorded as the date of the disappearance of the buffalo from the
Kiowa country. Thenceforth the appearance of even a single
animal was a rare event.—Mooney

In New Mexico the land is made of many colors. When I was
a boy I rode out over the red and yellow and purple earth
to the west of Jemez Pueblo. My horse was a small red roan,
fast and easy-riding. I rode among the dunes, along the bases of
mesas and cliffs, into canyons and arroyos. I came to know
that country, not in the way a traveler knows the landmarks he
sees in the distance, but more truly and intimately, in every
season, from a thousand points of view. I know the living motion
of a horse and the sound of hooves. I know what it is, on a
hot day in August or September, to ride into a bank of cold,
fresh rain.

a row of greased buffalo skulls.

XX

Once there was a man who owned a fine hunting horse. It was
black and fast and afraid of nothing. When it was turned upon an
enemy it charged in a straight line and struck at full speed; the
man need have no hand upon the rein. But, you know, that man
knew fear. Once during a charge he turned that animal from its
course. That was a bad thing. The hunting horse died of shame.

In 1861 a Sun Dance was held near the Arkansas River in Kansas. As an offering to Tai-me, a spotted horse was left tied to a pole in the medicine lodge, where it starved to death. Later in that year an epidemic of smallpox broke out in the tribe, and the old man Gaapiatan sacrificed one of his best horses, a fine black-eared animal, that he and his family might be spared.

I like to think of old man Gaapiatan and his horse. I think I know how much he loved that animal; I think I know what was going on in his mind: If you will give me my life and the lives of my family, I will give you the life of this black-eared horse.

XXI

Mammedaty was the grandson of Guipahgo, and he was well-known on that account. Now and then Mammedaty drove a team and wagon out over the plain. Once, in the early morning, he was on the way to Rainy Mountain. It was summer and the grass was high and meadowlarks were calling all around. You know, the top of the plain is smooth and you can see a long way. There was nothing but the early morning and the land around. Then Mammedaty heard something. Someone whistled to him. He looked up and saw the head of a little boy nearby above the grass. He stopped the horses and got down from the wagon and went to see who was there. There was no one; there was nothing there. He looked for a long time, but there was nothing there.

There is a single photograph of Mammedaty. He is looking past the camera and a little to one side. In his face there is calm and good will, strength and intelligence. His hair is drawn close to the scalp, and his braids are long and wrapped with fur. He wears a kilt, fringed leggings, and beaded moccasins. In his right hand there is a peyote fan. A family characteristic: the veins stand out in his hands, and his hands are small and rather long.

Mammedaty saw four things that were truly remarkable. This head of the child was one, and the tracks of the water beast another. Once, when he walked near the pecan grove, he saw three small alligators on a log. No one had ever seen them before and no one ever saw them again. Finally, there was this: something had always bothered Mammedaty, a small aggravation that was never quite out of mind, like a name on the tip of the tongue. He had always wondered how it is that the mound of earth which a mole makes around the opening of its burrow is so fine. It is nearly as fine as powder, and it seems almost to have been sifted. One day Mammedaty was sitting quietly when a mole came out of the earth. Its cheeks were puffed out as if it had been a squirrel packing nuts. It looked all around for a moment, then blew the fine dark earth out of its mouth. And this it did again and again, until there was a ring of black, powdery earth on the ground. That was a strange and meaningful thing to see. It meant that Mammedaty had got possession of a powerful medicine.

things that were truly remarkable.

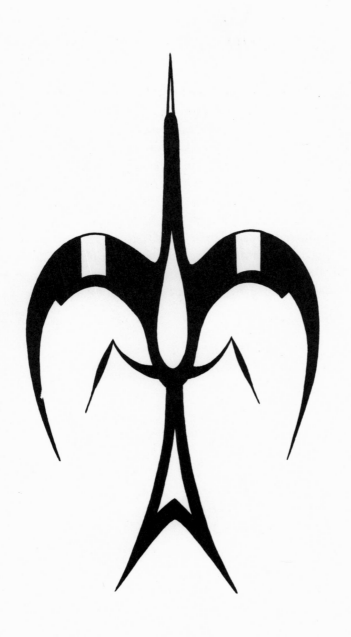

XXII

Mammedaty was the grandson of Guipahgo, and he got on well most of the time. But, you know, one time he lost his temper. This is how it was: There were several horses in a pasture, and Mammedaty wanted to get them out. A fence ran all the way around and there was just one gate. There was a lot of ground inside. He could not get those horses out. One of them led the others; every time they were driven up to the gate, that one wheeled and ran as fast as it could to the other side. Well, that went on for a long time, and Mammedaty burned up. He ran to the house and got his bow and arrows. The horses were running in single file, and he shot at the one that was causing all that trouble. He missed, though, and the arrow went deep into the neck of the second horse.

In the winter of 1852-53, a Pawnee boy who had been held as a captive among the Kiowas succeeded in running away. He took with him an especially fine hunting horse, known far and wide as Guadal-tseyu, "Little Red." That was the most important event of the winter. The loss of that horse was a hard thing to bear.

Years ago there was a box of bones in the barn, and I used to go there to look at them. Later someone stole them, I believe. They were the bones of a horse which Mammedaty called by the name "Little Red." It was a small bay, nothing much to look at, I have heard, but it was the fastest runner in that whole corner of the world. White men and Indians alike came from far and near to match their best animals against it, but it never lost a race. I have often thought about that red horse. There have been times when I thought I understood how it was that a man might be moved to preserve the bones of a horse—and another to steal them away.

the arrow went deep into the neck.

XXIII

Aho remembered something, a strange thing. This is how it was:
You know, the Tai-me bundle is not very big, but it is full of
power. Once Aho went to see the Tai-me keeper's wife. The two
of them were sitting together, passing the time of day, when they
heard an awful noise, as if a tree or some other very heavy object
had fallen down. It frightened them, and they went to see what on
earth it was. It was Tai-me—Tai-me had fallen to the floor. No one
knows how it was that Tai-me fell; nothing caused it, as far as anyone could see.

For a time Mammedaty wore one of the grandmother bundles. This he did for his mother Keahdinekeah; he wore it on a string tied around his neck. Aho remembered this: that if anyone who wore a medicine bundle failed to show it the proper respect, it grew extremely heavy around his neck.

There was a great iron kettle which stood outside of my grandmother's house next to the south porch. It was huge and immovable, or so I thought when I was a child; I could not imagine that anyone had strength enough to lift it up. I don't know where it came from; it was always there. It rang like a bell when you struck it, and with the tips of your fingers you could feel the black metal sing for a long time afterward. It was used to catch the rainwater with which we washed our hair.

XXIV

East of my grandmother's house, south of the pecan grove, there is buried a woman in a beautiful dress. Mammedaty used to know where she is buried, but now no one knows. If you stand on the front porch of the house and look eastward towards Carnegie, you know that the woman is buried somewhere within the range of your vision. But her grave is unmarked. She was buried in a cabinet, and she wore a beautiful dress. How beautiful it was! It was one of those fine buckskin dresses, and it was decorated with elk's teeth and beadwork. That dress is still there, under the ground.

Aho's high moccasins are made of softest, cream-colored skins. On each instep there is a bright disc of beadwork—an eight-pointed star, red and pale blue on a white field—and there are bands of beadwork at the soles and ankles. The flaps of the leggings are wide and richly ornamented with blue and red and green and white and lavender beads.

East of my grandmother's house the sun rises out of the plain. Once in his life a man ought to concentrate his mind upon the remembered earth, I believe. He ought to give himself up to a particular landscape in his experience, to look at it from as many angles as he can, to wonder about it, to dwell upon it. He ought to imagine that he touches it with his hands at every season and listens to the sounds that are made upon it. He ought to imagine the creatures there and all the faintest motions of the wind. He ought to recollect the glare of noon and all the colors of the dawn and dusk.

EPILOGUE

During the first hours after midnight on the morning of November 13, 1833, it seemed that the world was coming to an end. Suddenly the stillness of the night was broken; there were brilliant flashes of light in the sky, light of such intensity that people were awakened by it. With the speed and density of a driving rain, stars were falling in the universe. Some were brighter than Venus; one was said to be as large as the moon.

That most brilliant shower of Leonid meteors has a special place in the memory of the Kiowa people. It is among the earliest entries in the Kiowa calendars, and it marks the beginning as it were of the historical period in the tribal mind. In the preceding year Tai-me had been stolen by a band of Osages, and although it was later returned, the loss was an almost unimaginable tragedy; and in 1837 the Kiowas made the first of their treaties with the United States. The falling stars seemed to image the sudden and violent disintegration of an old order.

But indeed the golden age of the Kiowas had been short-lived, ninety or a hundred years, say, from about 1740. The culture would persist for a while in decline, until about 1875, but then it would be gone, and there would be very little material evidence that it had ever been. Yet it is within the reach of memory still, though tenuously now, and moreover it is even defined in a remarkably rich and living verbal tradition which demands to be preserved for its own sake. The living memory and the verbal tradition which transcends it were brought together for me once and for all in the person of Ko-sahn.

A hundred-year-old woman came to my grandmother's house one afternoon in July. Aho was dead; Mammedaty had died before I was born. There were very few Kiowas left who could remember the Sun Dances; Ko-sahn was one of them; she was a grown woman when my grandparents came into the world. Her body was twisted and her face deeply lined with age. Her thin white hair was held in place by a cap of black netting, though she wore braids as well, and she had but one eye. She was dressed in the manner of a Kiowa matron, a dark, full-cut dress that reached nearly to the ankles, full, flowing sleeves, and a wide, apron-like sash. She sat on a bench in the arbor so concentrated in her great age that she seemed extraordinarily small. She was quiet for a time —she might almost have been asleep—and then she began to speak and to sing. She spoke of many things, and once she spoke of the Sun Dance:

My sisters and I were very young; that was a long time ago.
Early one morning they came to wake us up. They had brought a
great buffalo in from the plain. Everyone went out to see and
to pray. We heard a great many voices. One man said that
the lodge was almost ready. We were told to go there, and
someone gave me a piece of cloth. It was very beautiful. Then
I asked what I ought to do with it, and they said that I must
tie it to the Tai-me tree. There were other pieces of cloth on the
tree, and so I put mine there as well.
When the lodge frame was finished, a woman—sometimes
a man—began to sing. It was like this:

> *Everything is ready.*
> *Now the four societies must go out.*
> *They must go out and get the leaves,*
> > *the branches for the lodge.*

And when the branches were tied in place, again there was
singing:

> *Let the boys go out.*
> *Come on, boys, now we must get the earth.*

The boys began to shout. Now they were not just ordinary boys,
not all of them; they were those for whom prayers had been
made, and they were dressed in different ways. There was
an old, old woman. She had something on her back. The boys
went out to see. The old woman had a bag full of earth on her
back. It was a certain kind of sandy earth. That is what they
must have in the lodge. The dancers must dance upon the sandy
earth. The old woman held a digging tool in her hand. She
turned towards the south and pointed with her lips. It was like
a kiss, and she began to sing:

> *We have brought the earth.*
> *Now it is time to play;*
> *As old as I am, I still have the feeling of play.*

That was the beginning of the Sun Dance. The dancers treated
themselves with buffalo medicine, and slowly they began
to take their steps . . . And all the people were around, and they
wore splendid things—beautiful buckskin and beads. The
chiefs wore necklaces, and their pendants shone like the sun.
There were many people, and oh, it was beautiful! That was the
beginning of the Sun Dance. It was all for Tai-me, you know,
and it was a long time ago.

It was—all of this and more—a quest, a going forth upon the way
to Rainy Mountain. Probably Ko-sahn too is dead now. At times,
in the quiet of evening, I think she must have wondered, dreaming,
who she was. Was she become in her sleep that old purveyor of
the sacred earth, perhaps, that ancient one who, old as she was,
still had the feeling of play? And in her mind, at times, did she
see the falling stars?

RAINY MOUNTAIN CEMETERY

Most is your name the name of this dark stone.
Deranged in death, the mind to be inheres
Forever in the nominal unknown,
The wake of nothing audible he hears
Who listens here and now to hear your name.

The early sun, red as a hunter's moon,
Runs in the plain. The mountain burns and shines;
And silence is the long approach of noon
Upon the shadow that your name defines—
And death this cold, black density of stone.

Typefaces used in this book are
Linotype Electra Roman and Oblique, 11 on 14,
and Optima Italic, 10 on 14, with titles handset
in Optima Roman.
Printed by offset on Warren's 66 Antique
and bound in Holliston Fabriqué.
Designed by Bruce Gentry.